Mums' Cakes & Slices

Carmel McCartin

Mums' Cakes & Slices

Published 2014 by Budget Bitch Australia

Copyright © 2014 Carmel McCartin

This book is copyright.

Editing & Formatting: Michael Betts

Publisher: Budget Bitch Pty Ltd

ABN 65 123 977 480

Kingston Road Thurgoona NSW 2640

Australia

www.BudgetBitch.com.au

ISBN: 0987511351
ISBN-13: 978-0-9875113-5-5

This is for my mother

Patricia Petrie

Thanks for the baking

A Recipe for Life

Make equal parts of faith and courage,
Mix well with a sense of humour,
Sprinkle with a few tears,
And a large helping of kindness to others.
Bake in a good natured oven,
And dust with laughter
Remove all pity for self,
Scrape away all self-indulgence
And serve in generous helpings

Take equal parts of faith & courage,
Mix well with a sense of humour,
Sprinkle with a few tears,
And a large helping of kindness to others.
Bake in a good natured oven
And dust with laughter
Remove all pity for self,
Scrape away all self-indulgence
And serve in generous helpings

All good wishes, Pat,
& best of Luck in the
kitchen –
– from Olga F. –

Acknowledgements

Recipes are often shared between family and friends. This book would never have been possible without the generosity of shared recipes from these ladies, many of whom have now passed away.

Olga Fleischer
Edna Opperman
Noela Taylor
Pat Dunlop
Mrs Dillon
Linda from the wool shop

The recipe that is not shared with others will soon be forgotten, but when it is shared, it will be enjoyed by future generations. – Unknown

Foreword

Born as a member of the Baby Boomer generation, I grew up in the 60s'. It was a time when families were large and bank balances were small. Like many others, my mother stayed at home and cooked for her family.

Money was in short supply but there was always enough food on the table thanks to her culinary efforts. Although she had eleven mouths to feed daily, she always cheerfully added another cup of water to the soup, to feed a guest.

We took our lunch to school or work and there was always a sweet treat 'to finish on'. Cakes and biscuits were always made at home and served to family and guests alike.

My mother never believed that she was a good cook; yet her biscuits, cakes and slices were legendary amongst family and friends. Visitors to our home were always offered an array of tempting home-baking.

The recipe book was black – a 1955 wedding gift from a work colleague, Olga Fleischer. Olga hand-wrote the first entry 'a recipe for life' in Old English Text. It's my privilege to share that recipe today.

As her eldest daughter, Mums' recipe book has now been passed to me. It's one of my treasures and it evokes many memories as I remember those happy times and recreate her favourite recipes.

I also look in the mirror and as I realise why I'm so fat – I wouldn't take away even one mouthful of those wonderful cakes or slices.

Conversion Tables

Temperature

Description	Fahrenheit	Celsius
	325°	160°
Moderately slow (325-350° F)	350°	180°
Moderate (350-375° F)	375°	190°
Moderately hot (375-400° F)	400°	200°
Hot (400-450° F)	425°	220°
	450°	230°

Volume

¼ teaspoon	1.25 mls
½ teaspoon	2.5 mls
1 teaspoon	5 mls
1 tablespoon (4 teaspoons)	20 mls
¼ cup (2 fl ozs)	60 mls
⅓ cup (2¾ fl ozs)	80 mls
½ cup (4 fl ozs)	125 mls
¾ cup (6 fl ozs)	180 mls
1 cup (8¾ fl ozs)	250 mls

Mass (Weight)

1 oz	30 gms
4 ozs (¼ lb)	125 gms
8 ozs (½ lb)	250 gms
12 ozs (¾ lb)	375 gms
16 ozs (1lb)	500 gms (0.5 kgs)

1 Anzac Crispies

Ingredients
2 cups John Bull Oats
1 scant cup flour
½ cup sugar
½ cup melted butter (4 ozs)
1 tablespoon Golden Syrup
2 tablespoons boiling water
1 teaspoon bi-carb soda
Pinch salt

Method
Mix oats, sugar, flour and melted butter.
Add the syrup
Lastly add the soda dissolved in the boiling water.
Drop by spoonful on cold greased sheets and bake in moderate oven 15-20 minutes.

2 Banana Cake

<u>Ingredients</u>
2 eggs
4ozs butter
4ozs sugar
8ozs Self Raising flour
½ teaspoon soda dissolved in 1 tablespoon milk
2 small bananas mashed together with a few drops of vanilla

<u>Method</u>
Cream the butter and sugar.
Add eggs one at a time.
Add bananas, milk and soda and lastly fold in flour.
Bake in a greased tin in moderate oven 45-50 minutes
Ice with lemon icing

3 Banana Loaf

Ingredients
8ozs (2 teacups) Self Raising Flour
Pinch salt
3ozs (½ teacup) sugar
2ozs butter
1 egg
1 teacup milk
1 – 1½ bananas
½ level teaspoon bi-carbonate soda

Method
Cream the butter and sugar.
Add egg and beat well.
Add milk, soda and the mashed banana.
Lastly, fold in the sifted flour and the salt.
Turn into an oblong greased tin and bake in a moderate oven 30 – 35 mins.

4 Boiled Fruit Cake

<u>Ingredients</u>
1 cup water
¼ lb. butter
2 eggs
1 lb. mixed fruit
Pinch of salt
1 teaspoon Carb soda
2 teaspoons spice
1 cup sugar
Few walnuts and a little vanilla
1 cup plain flour
1 cup Self Raising Flour

<u>Method</u>:
Put butter, water, sugar, fruit, carb soda and mixed spice in a saucepan and bring slowly to boil.

Then add well-beaten eggs and flour, vanilla & nuts.

Mix well together and pour into tin.

Put 2 layers of greased brown paper in and around the tin.

Bake in a moderate oven for 1½ hours.

This was the first fruitcake that we learned to bake. Mum said it was easy, inexpensive and we wouldn't be able to muck it up and waste the ingredients. I think I need to go back to this recipe.

5 Brownies (Noela)

<u>Ingredients</u>
¾ cup plain flour
1 cup sugar
5 dessertspoons cocoa
½ teaspoon salt
3ozs soft butter
2 unbeaten eggs
1 teaspoon vanilla

<u>Method</u>
Place all ingredients in a large bowl and beat for 2 minutes.
Then add ½ cup chopped nuts.
Place mixture in 11" x 7" cake pan.
Bake 30 – 40 minutes in moderate oven.

This recipe came from Mums' friend Noela Taylor. Easy to make, I was charged with the weekly baking of these from the age of 11 onwards. They were a staple component of our lunchboxes for many years. We found they were great to trade for tuck-shop items from kids whose mothers didn't bake.

6 Caramel Chews

<u>Ingredients</u>
3ozs brown sugar
4ozs white sugar
1 cup coconut
2 cups cornflakes
1 egg
4ozs Self Raising flour
½ teaspoon salt
3ozs copha
1 tablespoon milk

<u>Method</u>
Place in basin – brown sugar, white sugar, coconut, cornflakes, egg, sifted flour and salt.
Melt copha and add milk to copha.
Pour onto ingredients in basin.
Mix to combine evenly.
Place dessertspoonful on greased slides or paper cake containers.
Bake in moderate oven 12-15 minutes.

7 Caramel Fingers

<u>Ingredients</u>
½lb margarine
8 tablespoons brown sugar
2 eggs
½lb sultanas
½ teaspoon vanilla
3 cups Self Raising Flour – pinch salt

<u>Method</u>
Melt butter and brown sugar in saucepan to make a caramel sauce
Beat eggs, add vanilla and sultanas. Pour over melted butter and brown sugar.
Mix in flour.
Mix together with wooden spoon till all flour is mixed in.
Place in 2 trays
Bake in moderate oven for approx... 20-25 minutes.
Cut into squares while hot.

8 Caramel Walnut Slice

Ingredients
1 cup Self Raising Flour
1 cup coconut
½ cup castor sugar
125 grams butter, melted

Method
Grease lamington pan.
Combine sifted flour coconut & sugar.
Stir in butter
Press mixture into pan.
Bake in moderate oven for 15 minutes.
Spread topping and bake further 20 mins

Topping
2 eggs lightly beaten
1 teaspoon vanilla essence
1 cup coconut
¾ cup brown sugar, firmly packed
½ cup chopped walnuts

Combine eggs & essence in bowl
Stir in coconut, sugar, & walnuts
Mix well.

9 Carrot Loaf (Linda)

Ingredients
4ozs (½ cup) margarine
2 tablespoons golden syrup
¾ cup brown sugar
2 cups Kellogg's sultana bran
1½ cups Self Raising Flour; sifted well
½ teaspoon nutmeg & cinnamon
2 cups grated carrot
1 teaspoon vanilla
 2 eggs; lightly beaten

Method
Melt margarine, golden syrup and brown sugar in a saucepan over low heat, and then cool
Combine remaining ingredients in bowl
Stir in margarine mixture and mix till well combined
Place mixture in lined 24cm x 13 cm loaf tin
Bake at 190c for 1 – 1 ½ hours till cooked
Leave in tin for 5 minutes
Cool on wire rack
Serve in slices

This recipe came from Linda – a work colleague from the knitting shop where they both worked.

It was one of the first recipes for Mum that used metric measures. One can almost imagine these ladies giving baking advice as much as they did with wool and knitting patterns.

10 Choc Fruit Slice

<u>Ingredients</u>
1 cup mixed fruit (8ozs)
4ozs butter
½ teaspoon vanilla
½ cup castor sugar (4ozs)
2 eggs
4ozs S.R Flour
4ozs plain flour
3 dessertspoons cocoa
½ cup milk

<u>Method</u>
Cream butter, vanilla and sugar till mixture is light & creamy
Add egg & beat well
Add sifted flours and cocoa
Add mixed fruits
Spread mixture in slab tin and bake in moderate oven 20 minutes
Ice with <u>pink</u> icing & sprinkle with coconut while still warm

This was another regular lunchbox item, although it wasn't a favourite. We didn't like the fruit mixed with the chocolate nor the pink icing. It was, however, a hot item for trading.

11 Chocolate Fudge

Ingredients
1 heaped tablespoon cocoa
Knob of butter
1lb sugar
½ pint milk

Method
Pour milk into large saucepan & add the sugar.
Heat very gently over a low heat until the sugar has dissolved.
Bring to the boil and boil gently, stirring all the time, for 15 minutes
Be careful not to let the fudge boil over
Test a drop or 2 of the mixture in a cup of cold water to see if it forms a soft ball
If not continue boiling until it does.
Remove the pan from the heat and beat well. When the mixture thickens, pour it into a greased tin.
Leave in a cool place to set.
Mark into squares with a knife.

At the age of 12 this was the first recipe that I ever owned and I was so proud that it made it into Mums' Recipe Book.

Holidays and special occasions gave me reason to make this as it was a sweet rather than a cake.

12 Chocolate Lime Layer Cake

<u>Ingredients</u>
6ozs Self Raising Flour
6ozs castor sugar
3 level tabs cocoa
Pinch salt
3ozs melted butter
¾ cup milk
2 small eggs
Vanilla essence

<u>Method</u>
Place the flour, sugar, cocoa, vanilla and salt into a bowl.
Add the eggs
Heat the butter until it is just melted
Pour onto other ingredients & beat at medium speed for 2 minutes
Pour into 2 greased 7" sandwich tins and bake in moderate oven at 350°F for 25 – 30 mins
When cold, fill and ice with lime marshmallow frosting.

13 Christmas Cake (Edna)

<u>Ingredients</u>
4ozs brown sugar
4ozs castor sugar
1lb raisins
½ - 1lb currants
1lb sultanas
4ozs mixed peel
Cherries, dates walnuts
½ lb butter
4 tablespoons sherry or milk
8ozs plain flour
2ozs Self Raising Flour
¼ teaspoon salt
3 teaspoons spice

<u>Method</u>
Cream butter and sugar, add eggs then liquid. Sift flour, salt & spice. Mix half the flour mixture with the fruit then add ½ the fruit to egg mixture, then flour, then fruit etc.
<u>Bake</u> in a very moderate oven for 4 hours. (120º-150ºF gas, 3 hrs) (140ºF slow fan)
N.B. line tin with 2 layers of brown paper on top, sides & bottom & outside tin.

Quantity - 1½ for wedding cake (large tier)

Edna was Mums' cousin and she too was a great cook. As a tea-totaller Mum never added sherry or alcohol to the mix which didn't matter as the cake never lasted long enough to go mouldy or stale. She used this recipe for many wedding cakes and even without the alcohol I know of one top tier that lasted for five years.

14 Coconut Biscuits

Ingredients
¾ cup sugar
4ozs melted margarine
3 tabs boiling water
1 cup coconut
1 ½ cup Self Raising Flour

Method
Put sugar, melted margarine and boiling water in basin.
Add the coconut and flour.
Place teaspoonful on greased tray and bake in moderate oven 15 mins.

These biscuits made the school lunchboxes but were mostly kept in a special tin for visitors or Dads' late night suppers. They're easy to make and I still love them.

15 Coconut Delight (Noela Taylor)

<u>Ingredients</u>
1 cup Self Raising Flour
½ cup sugar
1 tablespoon cocoa
5ozs shortening
1 cup cornflakes
1 cup coconut
1 dessertspoon Golden Syrup
½ teaspoon vanilla

<u>Method</u>
Place in bowl flour, cocoa, coconut, lightly crushed cornflakes, sugar and vanilla.
Melt shortening and golden syrup, and add to dry ingredients
Press into a Swiss-roll tin and bake in moderate oven for 20 – 30 minutes.
Ice with chocolate icing and sprinkle with coconut.

16 Coffee Drops (Mrs Dillon)

<u>Ingredients</u>
1 tin Nestles Sweetened Condensed Milk
½ lb. coffee biscuits (morning coffee)
1 dessertspoon cocoa

<u>Method</u>
Crumb biscuits; mix well with cocoa to taste.
Add condensed milk.
Make into balls (1 teaspoon each).
Roll in coconut.
Set in fridge. (Makes about 60)

Mrs Dillon was the wife of an army officer who passed on the recipe after an Army Reserve social function. As kids, we didn't get to eat these, as coffee was considered bad for children.

As an adult – these are really yummy!

17 Cream Cheese Slice

<u>Ingredients</u>
1 pkt Lattice biscuits
4ozs pkt cream cheese
4ozs butter
½ cup castor sugar
1 teaspoon vanilla
2 teaspoons lemon juice
2 teaspoons gelatine dissolved in boiling water

<u>Method</u>
Cream cheese and butter well.
Gradually add sugar
Beat well; then add other ingredients
Place half biscuits in a flat tin (11" x 7" or smaller)
Spread mixture over, then put other half of biscuits on top
Leave to set
Ice with lemon icing.

This became a huge favourite during the 1980s' and many relatives still have fond memories of this recipe today. Mum made it for social occasions and family get-togethers.

18 Date & Walnut Loaf

Ingredients
2 cups Self Raising Flour
1 cup sugar
1 teaspoon carb soda
4 teaspoons cinnamon
1 cup chopped dates
1 cup chopped walnuts
2ozs butter
1⅓ cups water

Method
Mix all dry ingredients together
Heat butter & water in saucepan until water comes to boil
Pour into mixture & mix well
Bake in moderate oven approx. 40 mins

I remember making this often as a teenager. Sliced and spread with a little butter; it was regularly served to visitors for afternoon tea.

19 Date Loaf

<u>Ingredients</u>
1¾ cups Self Raising Flour
1 small cup sugar
1 cup stoned dates
2 tablespoons butter (or margarine)
1 teaspoon carb soda
Mixed spice, cinnamon to taste
1 egg
1 cup boiling water

<u>Method</u>
Put sugar, chopped stoned dates, butter, spice and cinnamon in mixing bowl. Over this, sprinkle carb soda and mix well.
Pour one cup of boiling water over these ingredients.
Stir well, until butter is dissolved and dates soft.
Add egg well beaten and stir in sifted flour.
Bake in moderate oven ¾ hour.

20 Fruit Bars (Noela)

Ingredients
¼ cup margarine
½ cup sugar
1 egg
½ cup treacle or Golden Syrup
½ cup milk
2 cups plain flour
1½ teaspoons baking powder
½ teaspoon bi-carb soda
1 cup chopped nuts
1 – 2 cup mixed fruit

Method
Blend butter, sugar, egg and treacle together thoroughly.
Stir in milk
Sift dry ingredients together and stir into mixture.
Mix in nuts and fruit
Spread into 2 greased biscuit slice trays
Bake in moderate oven for 30 – 40 minutes.

This also made an appearance in the school lunchbox although the amount of ingredients made it less cost effective than some others.

21 Fudge Cake

Ingredients
1½ cups Self Raising Flour
¼ cup melted butter (2½ ozs)
¼ cup boiling water
2 teaspoons cocoa
1 cup sugar
½ cup milk
1 egg
Salt

Method
Mix dry ingredients together
Make hole in centre and drop in milk butter, egg
and lastly water
Mix well
Bake in moderate oven 20 minutes
Ice with Vienna icing.

22 Hedgehog Cake

Ingredients
¼ lb. butter
½ cup sugar
½ cup walnuts (chopped)
1 egg
½ lb. broken biscuits
2 tablespoons cocoa

Method
Melt butter and sugar and cocoa in a saucepan.
Add biscuits, nuts and beaten eggs.
Pour into a greased tin to set (is quicker in fridge)
Ice with choc icing.

This recipe came from Olga Fleischer and was originally hand-written into the book

23 Iced Cream Cakes

Ingredients
6ozs Self Raising Flour
2ozs plain flour
Pinch of salt
4ozs butter
4ozs sugar
2 eggs
½ teacup milk
Lemon or vanilla essence

Method:
Cream butter and sugar, add eggs very slowly, beating well.
Mix in sifted flour and salt alternately with the milk and essence.
Place the mixture in fairly flat greased patty tins.
Bake in moderate oven 10-15 minutes.
When cold, ice with soft icing.
Cut a round cap from the centre of each cake. Fill the hole with whipped cream and replace the cap.

These were sometimes known as Patty Cakes because of the Patty Tins that they were baked in. Today, I often use this recipe for Cup Cakes.

24 Lemon Cake

Ingredients
3½ tablespoons of melted butter
2 eggs
1 cup white sugar
½ cup milk
1 cup Self Raising flour
1 cup icing sugar
1 lemon

Method:
Sift flour twice.

Combine remaining ingredients but leave out ½ oz. butter, the lemon and icing sugar.

Beat mixture for 2 minutes.

Pour into a greased tin (log tin) and bake in a moderate oven for ½ hour.

Make icing by stirring melted butter and as much of the juice of the lemon as will make a smooth paste with icing sugar.

25 Lemon Fingers

Ingredients
8ozs crushed sweet biscuits
3ozs coconut
½ can sweetened condensed milk
4ozs butter
Rind and juice of 1 lemon
1 ½ cups icing sugar

Method
Crush the biscuits with a rolling pin and add the coconut.
Melt the butter and add condensed milk.
Pour onto the biscuits and mix thoroughly
Pour into a greased 9" square tine and pour lemon icing over the top
Allow to set and cut into finger lengths.

This was an afternoon tea favourite for visitors. They're still a big hit in my household.

26 Lemon Ginger Biscuit Slice

<u>Ingredients</u>
4ozs butter or similar
4ozs sugar
2 level tablespoon coconut
1 tablespoon lemon juice
Grated rind of 1 lemon
1 beaten egg
¼ cup crystallised ginger
Approx. ½ lb crushed sweet biscuits

<u>Method</u>
Place the butter, sugar, coconut, and lemon juice in a saucepan and stir until well mixed.
Cook for 2 minutes
Remove from the heat and cool slightly,
Add the grated lemon rind, the beaten egg, chopped ginger and enough crushed biscuits to make a good consistency.
Spread in flat tin, like lamington tin, and when cool – ice with lemon icing.

27 Lime Frosting

<u>Ingredients</u>
1 cup sifted icing sugar
½ cup water
1 dessertspoon Gelatine
¼ cup lemon juice
Few drops green colouring
1 teaspoon lime essence
2 egg whites

<u>Method</u>
Dissolve the gelatine in the water.
Add the lemon juice and allow to partially set.
Beat egg whites stiffly then add gelatine mixture and icing sugar alternately, beating at high speed all the time
When it is becoming thick and spongy, add the green colouring and lime essence.
Use as a filling and topping for chocolate cake (chocolate Lime Layer Cake).

28 Milk Ice Blocks

<u>Ingredients</u>
¼ pint water
½ pint milk
2 tablespoons sugar

<u>Method</u>
Combine sugar and water in small saucepan and stir till sugar dissolves.
Boil for few minutes.
Allow to cool slightly
Add milk and dash vanilla essence
Pour into trays & freeze to set

This takes me back to hot summer days when I was a pre-schooler. I can still see us sitting on the edge of the canvas paddling pool, cooling our feet whilst sucking on these home-made ice-blocks.

29 Mocha Brownies

<u>Ingredients</u>
6ozs sugar
2 eggs
1 teaspoon vanilla
1 tablespoon coffee essence
5ozs Self Raising Flour
½ teaspoon salt
1 tablespoon cocoa
3ozs copha
½ cup chopped nuts or 1 cup mixed fruit

<u>Method</u>
Place in basin sugar, egg, vanilla, coffee essence and half sifted flour salt & cocoa.
Melt copha and pour onto ingredients then beat for 2 minutes.
Mix in remaining flour and nuts or fruit.
Place in a greased slab tin and bake in moderate oven.
Cut when cold, into squares or finger lengths and ice if desired.

30 Munchies

<u>Ingredients</u>
1 cup rolled oats
1 cup plain flour
1 cup sugar
1 cup coconut
1 tabs Golden Syrup
4ozs butter
1 teaspoon bi-carb soda
2 tabs boiling water

<u>Method</u>
Mix the oats, flour, sugar and coconut together.
Melt butter and Golden Syrup together.
Mix the soda with boiling water and add to the butter and syrup
Pour onto dry ingredients
Place teaspoonful onto greased trays – allow space for spreading
Bake in slow oven.

31 Orange Cake (Edna)

<u>Ingredients</u>
4ozs soft butter
½ cup milk
2 eggs
¾ cup castor sugar
1½ cups Self Raising Flour
1 tablespoon orange rind (grated)

<u>Method</u>
Combine all ingredients & beat for 3 minutes
Cook in moderate oven 30 – 40 mins
Ice with orange flavoured icing

32 Peanut Biscuits

<u>Ingredients</u>
4ozs butter or margarine
4ozs sugar
1 egg
Vanilla essence
3ozs peanuts
2 rounded teaspoons cocoa
Pinch salt
7ozs Self Raising Flour

<u>Method</u>
Cream together the margarine and sugar until light & fluffy.
Add the egg and vanilla essence and beat well
Add peanuts
Sift the cocoa, salt and flour and add to the creamed mixture mixing well. The mixture will be rather firm
Place teaspoonfuls on greased baking trays
Bake at 350°F for about 20 minutes.

This was another regular in the biscuit tin.

33 Peanut Brittle

<u>Ingredients</u>
3ozs sugar
1oz butter
1oz peanuts

<u>Method</u>
Boil together sugar and butter then add peanuts
Pour into a greased pan and allow mixture to set

This recipe comes from a time when sweet treats were made by mothers. With little time on their hands, is it any wonder this recipe is so simple?

34 Pineapple Fruit Cake

Place in large saucepan –
4ozs butter or margarine
15oz tin pineapple
12oz pkt mixed dried fruit
1 cup sugar
1 teaspoon mixed spice
1 teaspoon bi-carb soda

Simmer for 3 minutes and allow to cool

Stir in
2 cups Self Raising Flour
2 beaten eggs

Place in greased, lined 9" cake tin
Bake in moderate oven for 1½ hours
Check with clean fork, turn out when cool.

Pineapple fruit cake was hugely popular during the 1970s'. It was an era that turned 'the establishment' upside down and this recipe was written in a similar fashion. It was however, easy to make and quite yummy!

35 Rocky Mallow Slice

Ingredients
Crush 3 Weetbix finely
Add ¾ cups sugar
2 tablespoons cocoa
1 cup coconut
1 cup Self Raising Flour

Method
Add ¼lb melted copha and mix ingredients together
Press into greased tin
Bake in slow oven 10 – 12 minutes

Topping
Dissolve 2 dessertspoons gelatine in 1 cup boiling water
Pour over 2 cups sugar and beat until mixture is thick
Add vanilla essence and a few drops of cochineal.
Pour over biscuits
Leave until set and then cut into squares.

36 Simple Date & Walnut Slice

<u>Ingredients</u>
4ozs margarine (melted)
4ozs sugar
1 cup Self Raising Flour
1 cup chopped dates
½ cup walnuts (chopped)
1 egg

<u>Method</u>
Mix all ingredients together with the melted margarine and bake in greased slab tin until browned.
May be iced with lemon icing when cold

N.B. make a double quantity if you have a horde of kids to feed.

37 Simplicity Chocolate Cake

<u>Ingredients</u>
2 tablespoons butter or margarine
2 level tablespoons cocoa
1 cup Self Raising Flour
1 cup sugar
½ cup milk
2 eggs
½ teaspoon vanilla

<u>Method</u>
Melt the butter.
Put all the other ingredients into a large basin and pour the melted butter on top of them.
Beat really hard for 3 minutes.
Pour the mixture into a prepared tin, and bake in a moderate oven for about ¾ hour.
Ice with chocolate icing on top and sides, if desired.

This was so easy to make and never lasted long in our house. I remember making it often as a teenager, for a family treat on a Sunday afternoon.

38 Sultana Loaf

<u>Ingredients</u>
1 cup sultanas
½ cup sugar
1oz butter or margarine
½ cup water
1½ (6ozs) Self Raising Flour

Pinch salt
<u>Method</u>
Place the sultanas, sugar, butter and water in a saucepan. Bring to boil, stirring well
Remove from heat and allow to become cold
Add the egg and beat well.
Fold in sifted flour and salt
Turn into a well-greased and lined bar tin 8"x 3"
Bake at 350ºF for 40 – 45 minutes.
Allow to cool
Serve sliced with butter.

39 Tea Cake (Pat Dunlop)

Sieve scant cup sugar and good heaped cup of Self Raising Flour, pinch of salt.

In a cup – fill ⅓ with melted butter, put in an egg (whole) fill up with milk.

Pour into flour and sugar, beat and turn into tin.

Sprinkle cinnamon and sugar on top.

Bake in above moderate oven for approx. 20 minutes.

I remember this lady always seemed to be in a hurry. This recipe seems to be indicative of that. Nonetheless, it's quick, easy and delicious – which ticks all my boxes today.

40 Windmill Cake

1 sponge cake decorated with windmills made as follows:

Cut ¼ block of dairy-milk chocolate finely.
Put in a cup, and place in a saucepan of hot water to melt chocolate to a spreading consistency.
Grease kitchen paper and spread on the melted chocolate to an oblong shape – the length being equal to diameter of sponge.
Before the chocolate has quite set, cut into windmill sails.
Pipe cream thickly in centre of cake and round the edges at intervals.
Stand the chocolate sails all around the cake – about 8.
Sprinkle with coconut.
A touch of colour on white piping is attractive – try nuts and cherries.

About The Author

Carmel McCartin is an accomplished writer and speaker. Her articles have been published both online and in the print media. This is her fourth book.

She decided to compile this book as a tribute to her mother, Patricia Petrie, who always felt that her cooking ability was less than acceptable.

Carmel believes that her mothers' baking has given her a life-long sweet tooth and has been the cornerstone of many happy entertaining occasions.

She hopes that you will also share the recipes that have been the backbone of a large family for many generations.

www.ingramcontent.com/pod-product-compliance
Lightning Source LLC
Chambersburg PA
CBHW060723030426
42337CB00017B/2983